THE DOORS
LYRICS 1965-

OMNIBUS PRESS
LONDON · NEW YORK · SYDNEY

This Edition © Copyright 1992 Omnibus Press
(A division of Book Sales Limited)

Copyright © 1992 Omnibus Press
(A Division of Book Sales Limited)

Picture research by Dave Brolan.

ISBN 0.7119.2894.0
Order No. OP 46788

Exclusive distributors:
Book Sales Limited
8/9 Frith Street, London W1V 5TZ.
Music Sales Corporation
257 Park Avenue South, New York, NY 10010, USA.
Music Sales Pty Limited
120 Rothschild Avenue, Rosebery, NSW 2018, Australia.
To the Music Trade only:
Music Sales Limited
8/9 Frith Street, London W1V 5TZ, UK.

Printed in Great Britain by BPC Wheatons Ltd, Exeter

Picture credits: Joel Brodsky: 20, 37; LFI: 27, 41, 58, 65, 67, 69;
Pictorial Press: 9, 11, 13, 15, 17, 23, 29, 34/35, 45, 46, 49, 51, 55, 61,
63, 70, 75, 77; Barry Plummer: 79; Rex Features: 19, 25, 31, 33, 39, 53;
David Sygal: 73.

Every effort has been made to trace the copyright holders of the
photographs in this book but one or two were unreachable.
We would be grateful if the photographers concerned would contact us.

A catalogue record for this book is available from
the British Library.

CONTENTS

THE POETRY OF JIM MORRISON
4

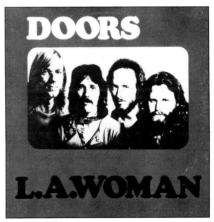

THE POETRY OF JIM MORRISON

Paris, May 1991: across the misty slopes of Père Lachaise cemetery, a series of simple hieroglyphics marks out a path. Every few yards, on one of the elaborate monuments that house the distinguished city dead, has been scrawled the word 'JIM', followed by an arrow pointing deeper into the maze of tombs. Within this shanty town of graves lie the remains of some of France's most fêted literary figures — Balzac and Molière, for example — together with dignitaries, politicians and aristocrats. Even Oscar Wilde is buried here, an honorary Frenchman welcomed as a fugitive from persecution at home.

Follow the 'JIM' trail up the hill, and you stumble upon a wake. The family of a civic notable pay silent tribute to their father, as part of a weekly ritual of remembrance. Heads bowed, they do their best to ignore the scene around them: twenty or thirty young men, plus a sprinkling of women, slumped across tombstones, or swaying in the cool morning drizzle. Apparently unaware of the genteel memorial service taking place beside them, these leather-jacketed worshippers clutch half-empty beer cans, a slipstream of empties at their feet; and they share the drunken chorus of a song that was briefly the voice of a generation, and is now — by the blessing of the great god Hollywood Hype — a rallying call for a more desperate, cynical era.

Their bacchanal surrounds a simple marble slab and headstone, which reads 'James Douglas Morrison'. Their song, chanted haphazardly in the uncertainty of a foreign language, pleads "C'mon baby, light my fire". On the tombstone they have lain dead flowers, and a funereal pyre of cans. Inside the tomb, which has been newly restored in preparation for the summer's soft parade of tourists, lie the mortal remains of a rock star, a shaman, a poet, a spiritual adventurer, a drunk, a transient idol who died with his reputation in decline, fat and half-forgotten three thousand miles from home.

The mourners of Jim Morrison represent one part of the man — the middle-class intellectual who cultivated the persona of an alcohol-scarred slob, the arrogant egotist who subjugated others' desires to his own whims. It was this Jim Morrison, celebrated in the million-selling biography by Jerry Hopkins and Danny Sugerman, who sent his tiny brother careering downhill on a sled towards a tree, who worked his way systematically through a queue of women as if they were inanimate playthings provided solely for his pleasure, who was seen (or so they thought) by thousands in the act of exposing himself onstage, and who died bloated and vomiting in his bath, a teen idol rotten with decay. It is this Morrison who brings followers to Père Lachaise, to lay the fitting tribute of an empty can of beer on his grave.

They have come in their thousands during the intervening twenty years since his death, and now the celebration of the wizard in Oliver Stone's hagiographical motion picture,"The Doors", has turned the trickle of visitors into a cascade. In an age light on youthful rebellion, Morrison's wilful path towards self-destruction has seen him reinvented as a god for the 1990s, the personification of every majestic enterprise and betrayed ideal thrown up by the more innocent decade in which he flourished.

The whole circus is tinged with irony. 1991 is the twentieth anniversary year — two decades being what it takes to translate pop culture reality into myth — but May is two months short of the actual date of his death. What the mourners are celebrating, whether they realise it or not, is not the death of a man, but the rebirth of a legend.

All history eventually becomes myth: in the twentieth century, the use of celluloid and video has simply hastened the process. Once, as Marx reminded us, those who ignored history were condemned to repeat it; now, as we near the end of the millenium, the process is reversed. Those who recall the past are now force-fed the re-runs, and as they watch the flickering images onscreen they are left to ponder why their own memories of events don't jell with the selective editing of the video historians. The development of history now begins in the cutting room: our view of our own past is limited by the collective vision imposed by the international media.

Jim Morrison would have recognised the dilemma. He was a student of the media, who found his own potential simultaneously inspired by the sense of possibility that they evoked, and dampened by their need to fix him into a single image frame. "Cinema is the most totalitarian of the arts," he wrote two years before his death, turning life into "a spectacle or a peep show". As a symbolist poet, Morrison shared the obsessive curiosity of the voyeur; as a spectacle in his own right, he felt the restrictive gaze of the public eye curtailing his experimentation with the limits of existence.

It is the public Morrison, driven to heights of exhibitionism by his urge to test the boundaries of consciousness and pleasure, who has survived as an icon. Like most public performers who endure the microscopic inspection of worldwide fame, he fabricated a persona to deflect attention from his inner being. And true to the norm, he gradually grew into his mask, and began to reflect that experience in his writings.

By itself, however, the public Morrison is a crinkled husk. It is given life only by the private man, the artist and thinker whose mental confusions fuelled the singer and the showman. Hundreds of young men in the age of the electronic media have assumed his form of stardom, bound up in the images of pioneers like James Dean, Marlon Brando and Elvis Presley. Exhibitionism is the easiest of the public arts to master: any fool (and many have done it) can strut across a stage, flaunt themselves suggestively in front of a camera, even pull out their penis on a Miami concert stage. What singles out Jim Morrison from, say, a Marc Bolan, is the mental process which supports and at the same time contradicts the conscious manipulation of the media. For Bolan and his ilk, stardom is an end in itself. For Morrison, it was a byproduct of his explorations into the maelstrom of artistic expression, and a means of conveying what he found to the outside world.

Ignore for a moment, if you can, the leather pants, the shamanistic writhings on stage, the surly demeanour of the natural rebel-hero: Jim Morrison's greatest artistic innovation was the translation of the methodology and inspiration of the French symbolist poets into the tight, rhythmic structures of rock music. Morrison was a creative artist before he ever sang in public; by the time The Doors were formed in 1965, he had already devoted four years to capturing the shadowy depths of his consciousness in fragmentary gems of poetry or prose. What The Doors provided was a link between the solitary life of the poet, and the outside world which was Morrison's playground.

Morrison's courageous experiment operated on dual stages. In public, through the lyrics included in this book, he sublimated the free-fall of imagery and expressionism to the strict format of the pop song. In private, for poetry and rhythmic prose which remained hidden in notebooks until after his death, or was occasionally exposed in small, unheralded limited editions for his friends, Morrison let loose his imagination.

What separated the two arenas is the awareness of foreign eyes. His song lyrics had to be manipulated to slot into the musical structures composed by the other members of The Doors. They required at least the trappings of universality, some sense that they offered shared experience rather than merely personal catharsis. Meanwhile, his private verse could range as far and as deeply as Morrison's in-built defence mechanisms would allow. Eventually, dulled by drugs and alcohol, all the barriers came down. For a moment, both in public and in private, Morrison's work flowed with the bittersweet rush of pure inspiration. Then, for the final year of his life, artistic control was swamped by chemical excess, and he set foot on the sorry path of despair and self-betrayal that led to the Paris bathroom, and to the initiation of the Jim Morrison death cult.

A gifted observer, like Morrison himself, perhaps, might have glimpsed a brief vision of his tortured progress in the role models which he chose as a fledgling poet. His artistic influences were typical enough in the late Fifties and early Sixties; his cocktail of romantic, doomed French poets, American explorers of the counter-culture, and Germanic philosophers of spiritual decays was the required reading of his artistic generation. As post-war materialism glibly satisfied the outer man, American teenagers switched their grail from survival of the body to the nurturing of the spirit. Middle-class life in America was an easy transition from one form of acquiescence to another; the path from college graduate to white-collar office worker led comfortably downhill, and it took a determined effort to overcome the laws of social gravity.

Morrison, like the rest of the so-called beat generation, was happy to accept the financial support of his family, but resented the assumptions that were part of the territory. He never rebelled against the charmed life of the student, tripping merrily from high school to college to university without the briefest hint that he might subvert the system. Within that cotton-wool security, however, he pushed his freedom to breaking point. Sometimes his experiment took the form of anti-social behaviour; more often he flew the flag of artistic innovation.

At high school, in his early teens, he discovered Fifties icons like Jack Kerouac and Allen Ginsberg. In radically different ways, this pair of friends and rivals extended the boundaries of what could be treated as poetry. Kerouac aimed for the heart, appealing to that eternal spark of adolescence that is fired by idealism and dissatisfaction with the conventions of everyday life. While Kerouac's fictional characters followed Twain's Huckleberry Finn in searching for some other territory that might contain them, Ginsberg compressed years of classical learning, political sensibility and drug-fuelled imagery into long outpourings of rhythm and verse, a solid howl of protest and imagination.

Together, Kerouac, Ginsberg and their disciples in the beat movement provided a heady example for any young writer. In Morrison, as in Bob Dylan and Lou Reed, they triggered a love of words, a desire for extremes, and a fearless refusal to be contained. These urges were then channelled and structured when Jim discovered the poetry of Rimbaud, Verlaine and Baudelaire, whose tight, formal verses mixed ferocious discipline with sensual, vivid imagery. Arthur Rimbaud, in particular, acted as a model: dead some seventy years when Morrison entered college, his work trumpeted complete disorganisation of the senses, a triumph of the unconscious mind over timidity and bourgeois self-control. At college, Morrison was once approached to play the role of Rimbaud in a class movie short. Even then, it must have struck him as typecasting.

Under the fiery influence of these literary adventurers, Morrison filled notebook after notebook with translations from his unconscious. Adopting the style he would maintain for the rest of his career as a poet, he wrote in dense, elliptical

6

phrases, sometimes linked in prose, more often left to swim together in a sea of oblique imagery. His work occasionally took on the semblance of some recognisable reality, though it could just as easily drift into the void.

Morrison always had grand designs — his initial conception of a mighty thematic work called "The Celebration Of The Lizard" dates back to his years at college in the early Sixties — but his execution was usually fragmentary in the extreme. Even here he had a mentor, in Friedrich Nietzsche, the German philosopher and imaginative writer whose collections of aphorisms and images, linked by a common vision rather than a narrative form, were the obvious precursors of mature Morrison works like "The Lords" and "The New Creatures". Both those books, originally issued shortly before Morrison's death in hand-bound limited editions, were subsequently reprinted as if they were long, continuous, interlinked works. As their original publication makes clear, Morrison intended each fragment of a thought or an idea to stand alone, as food for contemplation. Nietzsche's often baffling later works were an obvious exemplar for Morrison's own collections.

At Florida State University in the early Sixties, Morrison found an additional context for his experiments in free verse. He began to study the philosophy of protest, and discovered that his inner delvings could have a social purpose. Then he investigated the psychology of the crowd, learning the arts of manipulation and control, and pursuing notions of a universal consciousness which the canny artist could tap for his own ends.

Finally, he became involved in theatre, using his new-found knowledge of audience preconceptions to elicit the desired emotional responses. He began as a designer of scenery, providing startlingly savage backdrops for absurdist dramas. Then, after he moved to the UCLA film school in 1964, he devoted himself to staging his own visions, rather than colouring those of other people.

The final ingredient in this artistic education was provided by the element of chance — as exemplified by the haphazard inspiration of hallucinogenic chemicals, notably everyman's route to instant nirvana in the mid-Sixties, the acid trip.

LSD facilitated the probing of the unconscious that had previously been unlocked only by determined artistic exploration. Morrison's awareness of what motivated an audience, coupled with his delving into his own psyche, convinced him of the power of certain timeless symbols, touchstones for the experience of being human. These he began to incorporate into his work, providing the themes that fuelled not only his private poetry, but also the songs of The Doors. The same images recurred again and again — the fear of night's blackness as a metaphor for the terror of death, for instance, the fascination with the primaeval power of reptiles ("I am the lizard king/I can do anything", remember), and the belief that everyday life was separated from the riches of the unconscious by a wall, which required violent (drug-fuelled?) effort to tear down.

In the process, Morrison began to mythologise himself. "In the seance, the shaman led", he wrote in "The Lords". "He acts like a madman. These professional hysterics, chosen precisely for their psychotic leaning, were once esteemed. They mediated between man and spirit-world. Their mental travels formed the crux of the religious life of the tribe." A professional hysteric, a psychotic, a shaman: this was the role which Morrison took upon himself, which unlocked the poetry of The Doors' lyrics, and which dragged him inevitably into burn-out and eventually death.

As a lyricist, however, Morrison was much more than simply a vehicle for acid-tinged fantasies to reach the surface. Rock in the Sixties was a haven for would-be poets who discovered the divine through a tab of acid. Only those with poetic judgement were able to shape the random access of bizarre images thrown up by the acid experience into any form of sense.

Morrison had the poetic skills, and the commanding overall vision, to twist his drug psychosis into poetry. He was the first rock writer to give teenage rock music the intensely personal, opaque imagery of the symbolists. Bob Dylan is customarily credited as rock's first poet, but he never approached Morrison's blind trust in the workings of the unconscious. Dylan's imagery conveyed a sense of the world; in Morrison's best work, you can explore the subliminal, fundamental workings of the human psyche.

Morrison functioned best in momentary flashes of inspiration, which is why he adopted Nietzsche's canonisation of the fragment. "I see first lots of things which dance . . . then everything becomes gradually connected", he wrote in 1968, and the process of connection is not always apparent on the page. For every perfect union of thought and emotion like "Horse Latitudes", there is a "Soft Parade", which reads like a random sampling of Morrison's episodic notebook entries.

The link, unheard in the printed word but inescapable to anyone who is familiar with the songs, is provided by the music of The Doors. They stretched their instrumental framework in sympathy with Morrison's lyrics, maintaining a tightly traditional setting for his more orthodox songs, but extending almost free-form when presented with a primal flow of images and scenes like "The End" and "When The Music's Over". These works are unique in rock history. Most extended rock performances are determined by instrumental virtuosity, with their structure reflecting the interplay between the musicians, in the style of be-bop jazz or Chicago blues. The Doors could do that as well as the next California band, as "Roadhouse Blues" and "L.A. Woman" demonstrate. But in "The End" and "When The Music's Over", the structure of the music is defined by the direction of the words. Morrison's lyrics set the mood, for ten or twelve minutes, and The Doors respond to each change of emphasis, each switch of voice or perspective. To that extent, The Doors were Morrison's band; without him, as they proved after his death, they lacked that single unifying consciousness which mapped out the parameters of their music.

The same overpowering sense of self which guided Morrison's writing also fuelled his public appearances, and in turn set in motion the mythmaking which brings followers to Père Lachaise, and film-makers to re-create his life on celluloid. Morrison was an intoxicating — sometimes intoxicated, for that matter — stage performer, and his visual image survives in its own right, without any artistic justification. Partly, it was the sheer exhibitionism of the egotist which sent Morrison rampaging across the stage; and partly it was a desperate attempt to match the reckless psychological excavations of his poetry. For Jim Morrison, there was no gap between inspiration, creativity and performance. He lived life to the hilt, even when he couldn't control it. What he could control was his poetry and his lyrics, and it is there that he came closest to satisfying the demons set loose by his fearless investigation of his own psyche.

Break On Through

The Doors

You know the day destroys the night,
Night divides the day;
Tried to run,
Tried to hide.
Break on through to the other side,
Break on through to the other side,
Break on through to the other side.

We chased our pleasures here,
Dug our treasures there,
Can you still recall
The time we cried?
Break on through to the other side,
Break on through to the other side,
Break on through to the other side.

Ev'rybody loves my baby.
Ev'rybody loves my baby.

She gets, she gets,
She gets, she gets.

I found an island in your arms,
A country in your eyes,
Arms that chain,
Eyes that lie.
Break on through to the other side,
Break on through to the other side,
Break on through to the other side.

Made the scene from week to week,
Day to day, hour to hour,
The gate is straight,
Deep and wide.
Break on through to the other side,
Break on through to the other side,
Break on through to the other side.

Break on through, break on through,
Break on through, break on through.

Break, break,
Break, break,
break.

Soul Kitchen

The Doors

Well, the clock says it's time to close, now,
I guess I'd better go now,
I'd really like to stay here all night.

The cars crawl past all stuffed with eyes,
Street lights shed their hollow glow;
Your brain seems bruised with numb surprise.

Still one place to go,
Still one place to go.

Let me sleep all night in your soul kitchen,
Warm my mind near your gentle stove,
Turn me out and I'll wander, baby,
Stumbling in the neon groves.

Your fingers weave quick minarets,
Speak in secret alphabets
I light another cigarette,
Learn to forget, learn to forget,
Learn to forget, learn to forget.

Let me sleep all night in your soul kitchen,
Warm my mind near your gentle stove,
Turn me out and I'll wander, baby,
Stumbling in the neon groves.

Well, the clock says it's time to close, now,
I guess I'd better go now, I know I have to go, now,
I really want to stay here all night,
All night,
All night.

Twentieth Century Fox

The Doors

Well, she's fashionably lean,
And she's fashionably late,
She'll never rank a scene,
She'll never break a date;
But she's no drag,
Just watch the way she walks.

She's a twentieth century fox,
She's a twentieth century fox.

No tears, no fears,
No ruined years.
No clocks.
She's a twentieth century fox.

She's the queen of cool,
And she's the lady who waits,
Since her mind left school,
It never hesitates;
She won't waste time
On elementary talk.

'Cause she's a twentieth century fox,
She's a twentieth century fox.

Got the world locked up
Inside a plastic box.
She's a twentieth century fox, yeah,
Twentieth century fox.
Twentieth century fox, oh yeah!
She's a Twentieth century fox!

The Crystal Ship

The Doors

Before you slip into unconsciousness,
I'd like to have another kiss,
Another flashing chance at bliss,
Another kiss,
Another kiss.

The days are bright and filled with pain,
Enclose me in your gentle rain,
The time you ran was too insane,
We'll meet again,
We'll meet again.

Oh tell me where your freedom lies,
The streets are fields that never die,
Deliver me from reasons why
You'd rather cry,
I'd rather fly.

The crystal ship is being filled,
A thousand girls, a thousand thrills,
A million ways to spend your time;
When we get back,
I'll drop a line.

13

I Looked At You

The Doors

I looked at you,
You looked at me,
I smiled at you,
You smiled at me.

And we're on our way,
No, we can't turn back, babe;
Yeah, we're on our way,
And we can't turn back,
'cause it's too late,
Too late, too late,
Too late, too late.

And we're on our way,
No, we can't turn back, babe;
Yeah, we're on our way,
And we can't turn back.

I walk with you,
You walk with me,
I talked to you,
You talked to me.

And we're on our way,
No, we can't turn back, babe;
Yeah, we're on our way,
And we can't turn back.
'cause it's too late,
Too late, too late,
Too late, too late.

And we're on our way,
No, we can't turn back, babe;
Yeah, we're on our way,
And we can't turn back.
'cause it's too late,
Too late, too late,
Too late, too late.

14

Light My Fire

The Doors

You know that it would be untrue,
You know that I would be a liar,
If I was to say to you,
Girl we couldn't get much higher.

Come on, baby, light my fire,
Come on, baby, light my fire,
Try to set the night on fire.

The time to hesitate is through,
No time to wallow in the mire,
Try now we can only lose,
And our love become a funeral pyre.

Come on, baby, light my fire,
Come on, baby, light my fire,
Try to set the night on fire.

The time to hesitate is through,
No time to wallow in the mire,
Try now we can only lose,
And our love become a funeral pyre.

15

Come on, baby, light my fire,
Come on, baby, light my fire,
Try to set the night on fire.
Try to set the night on fire.
Try to set the night on fire.
Try to set the night on fire.

Take It As It Comes

The Doors

Time to live,
Time to lie,
Time to laugh,
Time to die.

Take it easy, baby,
Take it as it comes.
Don't move too fast if you want your love to last,
You've been movin' much too fast.

Time to walk,
Time to run,
Time to aim your arrows
At the sun.

Take it easy, baby,
Take it as it comes.
Don't move too fast if you want your love to last,
You've been movin' much too fast.

Go real slow,
You'll like it more and more,
Take it as it comes,
Specialize in havin' fun.

Take it easy, baby,
Take it as it comes,
Don't move too fast if you want your love to last,
You've been movin' much too fast,
Movin' much too fast,
Movin' much too fast.

End Of The Night

The Doors

Take the highway to the end of the night,
End of the night,
End of the night.
Take a journey to the bright midnight,
End of the night,
End of the night.

Realms of bliss,
Realms of light.
Some are born to sweet delight,
Some are born to sweet delight.
Some are born to the endless night.

End of the night,
End of the night,
End of the night,
End of the night.

Realms of bliss,
Realms of light,
Some are born to sweet delight,
Some are born to sweet delight.
Some are born to the endless night.

End of the night,
End of the night,
End of the night,
End of the night.

17

The End

The Doors

This is the end, beautiful friend,
This is the end, my only friend,
The end of our elaborate plans,
The end of ev'rything that stands,
The end.

No safety or surprise,
The end,
I'll never look into your eyes again.

Can you picture what will be,
So limitless and free,
Desperately in need of some stranger's hand,
In a desperate land.

Lost in a Roman wilderness of pain,
And all the children are insane,
All the children are insane;
Waiting for the summer rain,
There's danger on the edge of town,
Ride the king's highway.
Weird scenes inside the gold mine;
Ride the highway west, baby.

Ride the snake,
Ride the snake.
To the lake,
To the lake.

The ancient lake, baby,
The snake is long,
Seven miles,
Ride the snake.

He's old,
And his skin is cold.
The West is the best,
The West is the best.
Get here and we'll do the rest.

The blue bus is calling us,
The blue bus is calling us.
Driver, where are you taking us?

The killer awoke before dawn,
He put his boots on,
He took a face from the ancient gallery,
And he walked on down the hall.

He went to the room where his sister lived,
And then he paid a visit to his brother,
And then he walked on down the hall.

And he came to a door,
And he looked inside;
"Father?"
"Yes, son?"
"I want to kill you.
Mother, I want to..."

Come on, baby, take a chance with us
Come on, baby, take a chance with us
Come on, baby, take a chance with us
And meet me at the back of the blue bus.
Blue rah, round the...
Do the, blue bus,
Do the...
C'mon, yeah...
Yeah, yeah,
Yeah, yeah,
Yeah, yeah.

This is the end, beautiful friend.
This is the end, my only friend,
The end.

It hurts to set you free,
But you'll never follow me.

The end of laughter and soft lies,
The end of nights we tried to die.

This is the end.

Hello I Love You (Won't You Tell Me Your Name?)

The Doors

Hello, I love you,
Won't you tell me your name?
Hello, I love you,
Let me jump in your game.
Hello, I love you,
Won't you tell me your name?
Hello, I love you,
Let me jump in your game.

She's walkin' down the street,
Blind to ev'ry eye she meets,
Do you think you'll be the guy
To make the queen of the angels sigh?

Hello, I love you,
Won't you tell me your name?
Hello, I love you,
Let me jump in your game.
Hello, I love you,
Won't you tell me your name?
Hello, I love you,
Let me jump in your game.

She holds her head so high,
Like a statue in the sky,
Her arms are wicked and her legs are long,
When she moves my brain screams out this song.

Sidewalk crouches at her feet,
Like a dog that begs for something sweet.
Do you hope to make her see, you fool?
Do you hope to pluck this dusky jewel?
Hello,
Hello,
Hello,
Hello,
Hello,
Hello,
Hello,
I want you.
I need you.
Love.
Love.
Hello,
Hello,
Hello.

Love Me
Two Times

The Doors

Love me two times, baby,
Love me twice today,
Love me two times, girl,
I'm goin' away.

Love me two times, girl,
One for tomorrow,
One just for today;
Love me two times,
I'm goin' away.

Love me one time,
Could not speak.
Love me one time,
Yeah, my knees got weak.

Love me two times, girl,
Last me all through the week,
Love me two times,
I'm goin' away,
Love me two times,
I'm goin' away,
Oh yeah.

Love me one time,
Could not speak.
Love me one time,
Yeah, my knees got weak.

Love me two times, girl
Last me all through the week,
Love me two times,
I'm goin' away,
Love me two times,
I'm goin' away
Oh yeah.

Love me two times, baby,
Love me twice today,
Love me two times, girl,
I'm goin' away.

Love me two times, girl,
One for tomorrow,
One just for today;
Love me two times,
I'm goin' away.

Love me two times, baby,
Love me twice today,
Love me two times, girl,
I'm goin' away.

You're Lost, Little Girl

The Doors

You're lost, little girl,
You're lost, little girl,
You're lost,
Tell me who you are.

Think that you know what to do,
Impossible yes,
But it's true.

I think that you know what to do,
Yeah,
Sure that you know what to do.

You're lost, little girl,
You're lost, little girl,
You're lost,
Tell me who you are.

Think that you know what to do,
Impossible yes,
But it's true.

I think that you know what to do,
Girl,
Sure that you know what to do.

You're lost, little girl,
You're lost, little girl,
You're lost.

Moonlight Drive

The Doors

Let's swim to the moon,
Uh huh,
Let's swim thru the tide,
Penetrate the evenin' that the city sleeps to hide.

Let's swim out tonight, love,
It's our turn to try,
Parked beside the ocean
On our moonlight drive.

Let's swim to the moon,
Uh huh,
Let's climb thru the tide,
Surrender to the waiting worlds that lap against our side.

Nothin' left open
And no time to decide,
We've stepped into a river
On our moonlight drive.

Let's swim to the moon,
Let's climb thru the tide,
You reach a hand to hold me
But I can't be your guide.

Easy, I love you as I watch you glide,
Falling through wet forests
On our moonlight drive,
Moonlight drive.

Horse Latitudes

Jim Morrison

When the still sea conspires an armor
And her sullen and aborted
Currents breed tiny monsters,
True sailing is dead.

Awkward instant
And the first animal is jettisoned,
Legs furiously pumping
Their stiff green gallop,
And heads bob up
Poise
Delicate
Pause
Consent
In mute nostril agony
Carefully refined
And sealed over.

Love Street

The Doors

She lives on Love Street,
Lingers long on Love Street,
She has a house and garden,
I would like to see what happens.

She has robes and she has monkeys,
Lazy diamond studded flunkies,
She has wisdom and knows what to do,
She has me and she has you.

She has wisdom and knows what to do,
She has me and she has you.

She has wisdom and knows what to do,
She has me and she has you.

I see you live on Love Street,
There's the store where the creatures meet.
I wonder what they do in there,
Summer Sunday and a year.
I guess I like it fine so far

She lives on Love Street,
Lingers long on Love Street.
She has a house and garden,
I would like to see what happens.

La, la, la, la, la, la,
La, la, la, la, la, la,
La, la, la, la, la, la,
La, la, la, la, la, la,
La, la, la, la, la, la,

Strange Days

The Doors

Strange days have found us,
Strange days have tracked us down,
They're goin' to destroy our casual joys,
We shall go on playing or find a new town.

Strange eyes fill strange rooms,
Voices will signal their tired end,
The hostess is grinning,
Her guests sleep from sinning,
Hear me talk of sin and you know this is it.

Strange days have found us,
And through their strange hours,
We linger alone,
Bodies confused,
Memories misused,
As we run from the day,
To a strange night of stone.

People Are Strange

The Doors

People are strange when you're a stranger,
Faces look ugly when you're alone,
Women seem wicked when you're unwanted,
Streets are uneven when you're down.

When you're strange,
Faces come out of the rain,
When you're strange,
No one remembers your name.

When you're strange,
When you're strange,
When you're strange.

People are strange when you're a stranger,
Faces look ugly when you're alone,
Women seem wicked when you're unwanted,
Streets are uneven when you're down.

When you're strange,
Faces come out of the rain,
When you're strange,
No one remembers your name.

When you're strange,
When you're strange,
When you're strange.

Unhappy Girl

The Doors

Unhappy girl,
Left all alone,
Playin' solitaire,
Playin' warden to your soul;
You are locked in a prison of your own device.
And you can't believe what it does to me
To see you cryin'.

Unhappy girl,
Tear your web away,
Saw thru' all your bars,
Melt yourself today;
You are caught in a prison of your own device.

Unhappy girl,
Fly fast away,
Don't miss your chance
To swim in mystery;
You are dying in a prison of your own device.

My Eyes Have Seen You

The Doors

My eyes have seen you,
My eyes have seen you,
My eyes have seen you
Stand in your door,
Meet inside,
Show me some more,
Show me some more,
Show me some more.

My eyes have seen you,
My eyes have seen you,
My eyes have seen you
Turn and stare,
Fix your hair,
Move upstairs,
Move upstairs,
Move upstairs.

My eyes have seen you,
My eyes have seen you,
My eyes have seen you
Free from disguise,
Gazing on a city
Under television skies,
Television skies,
Television skies.

My eyes have seen you,
My eyes have seen you,
Eyes have seen you,
Let them photograph your soul,
Memorize your alleys
On an endless roll,
Endless roll,
Endless roll,
Endless roll.

(repeat to fade)

I Can't See
Your Face

The Doors

I can't see your face in my mind,
I can't see your face in my mind,
Carnival dogs consume the lines,
Can't see your face in my mind.

Don't you cry,
Baby,
Please don't cry,
And don't look at me with your eyes.

I can't seem to find the right lie,
I can't seem to find the right lie.

Insanity's horse adorns the sky,
Can't seem to find the right lie.

Carnival dogs consume the lines,
Can't see your face in my mind.

Don't you cry,   31
Baby,
Please don't cry,
I won't need your picture
Until we say goodbye.

When The Music's Over

The Doors

Yeah,
When the music's over,
When the music's over here,
When the music's over,
Turn out the lights,
Turn out the lights,
Turn out the lights,
Yeah, yeah.

When the music's over,
When the music's over,
When the music's over,
Turn out the lights,
Turn out the lights,
Turn out the lights.

For the music is your special friend,
Dance on fire as it intends,
Music is your only friend,
Until the end,
Until the end,
Until the end.

Cancel my subscription to the resurrection,
Send my credentials to the house of detention,
I got some friends inside.

The face in the mirror won't stop,
The girl in the window won't drop,
A feast of friends alive she cried,
Waiting for me outside.

Before I sink into the big sleep,
I want to hear,
I want to hear,
The scream of the butterfly.

Come back, baby,
Back into my arms.

We're getting tired of hangin' around,
Waiting around,
With our heads to the ground.

I hear a very gentle sound,
Very near,
Yet very far,
Very soft,
Yet very clear.
Come today,
Come today.

What have they done to the earth?
What have they done to our fair sister?

Ravaged and plundered,
And ripped her,
And bit her,
Stuck her with knives
In the side of the dawn,
And tied her with fences,
And dragged her down.

I hear a very gentle sound,
With your ear down to the ground –
We want the world and we want it,
We want the world and we want it,
Now!

Persian night! Babe,
See the light! Babe,
Save us!
Jesus!
Save us!

So when the music's over,
When the music's over, yeah,
When the music's over, yeah,
Turn out the light,
Turn out the light.

33

For the music is your special friend,
Dance on fire as it intends,
Music is your only friend,
Until the end,
Until the end,
Until the end.

So when the music's over,
When the music's over, yeah,
When the music's over, yeah,
Turn out the light,
Turn out the light.

Not To Touch
The Earth

The Doors

Not to touch the earth,
Not to see the sun,
Nothing left to do but run run run,
Let's run,
Let's run.

House upon the hill,
Moon is lying still,
Shadows of the trees,
Witnessing the wild breeze.
Come on, baby, run with me,
Let's run.

Run with me,
Run with me,
Run with me,
Let's run.

The mansion is warm at the top of the hill,
Rich are the rooms and the comforts there.
Red are the arms of luxuriant chairs,
And you won't know a thing till you get inside.

Dead President's corpse in the driver's car,
The engine runs on glue and tar,
Come on along, not goin' very far,
To the East to meet the Czar.

Run with me,
Run with me,
Run with me,
Let's run.

Some outlaws live by the side of a lake,
The minister's daughter's in love with the snake,
Who lives in a well by the side of the road,
Wake up, girl, we're almost home.

Sun, sun, sun
Burn, burn, burn
Soon, soon, soon
Moon, moon, moon,
I will get you
Soon!
Soon!
Soon!

Let the carnival bells ring
Let the serpent sing
Let everything

We came down
The rivers and highways
We came down from
Forests and falls

We came down from
Carson and Springfield
We came down from
Phoenix enthralled
And I can tell you
The names of the kingdom
I can tell you
The things that you know
Listening for a fistful of silence
Climbing valleys into the shade.

Wintertime Love

The Doors

Wintertime winds blow cold this season,
Fallin' in love I'm hopin' to be,
Wind is so cold,
Is that the reason,
Keeping you warm, your hands touching me.

Come with me,
Dance, my dear,
Winter's so cold this year.
You are so warm,
My wintertime love to be.

Wintertime winds blue and freezin'
Comin' from northern storms in the sea,
Love has been lost,
Is that the reason,
Trying so desperately to be free.

Come with me,
Dance, my dear,
Winter's so cold this year.
You are so warm,
My wintertime love to be.

Come with me,
Dance, my dear,
Winter's so cold this year.
You are so warm,
My wintertime love to be.

Summer's Almost Gone

The Doors

Summer's almost gone,
Summer's almost gone,
Almost gone,
Yeah,
It's almost gone.

Where will we be
When the summer's gone?

Morning found us calmly unaware,
Noon burned gold into our hair,
At night we swam the laughin' sea.

When summer's gone,
Where will we be?
Where will we be?
Where will we be?

Morning found us calmly unaware,
Noon burned gold into our hair,
At night we swam the laughin' sea.

When summer's gone,
Where will we be?

Summer's almost gone,
Summer's almost gone.
We had some good times
But they're gone.

The winter's coming on,
Summer's almost gone.

We Could Be So Good Together

The Doors

We could be so good together,
Yeah, so good together,
We could be so good together,
Yeah, we could,
I know we could.

Tell you lies,
I'll tell you wicked lies,
Tell you lies,
Tell you wicked lies.

I tell you 'bout the world that we'll invent,
Wanton world without lament,
Enterprise, expedition,
Invitation and invention.

Yeah,
So good together,
Ah, so good together,
We could be so good together,
Yeah, we could,
Know we could.

We could be so good together,
Yeah, so good together,
We could be so good together,
Yeah, we could,
Know we could.

Tell you lies,
Tell you wicked lies,
Tell you lies,
Tell you wicked lies.

The time you wait subtracts from joy,
Beheads the angels you destroy;
Angels fight,
Angels cry,
Angels dance and Angels die.

We could be so good together,
Yeah, so good together,
We could be so good together,
Yeah, we could,
I know we could.

Spanish Caravan

The Doors

Carry me,
Caravan,
Take me away,
Take me to Portugal,
Take me to Spain,
Andalusia,
With fields full of grain.

I have to see you
Again and again.
Take me,
Spanish caravan,
Yes,
I know you can.

Tradewind galleons,
Lost in the sea,
I know a treasure,
Is waiting for me.
Silver and gold,
In the mountains of Spain.

I have to see you
Again and again.
Take me,
Spanish caravan,
Yes,
I know you can.

Five To One

The Doors

Five to one, baby,
One in five,
No one here gets out alive.
Now,
You get yours, baby,
I'll get mine,
Gonna make it, baby,
If we try.

The old get old and the young get stronger,
May take a week and it may take longer,
They got the guns but we got the numbers,
Gonna win,
Yeah, we're takin' over,
Come on.

Your ballroom days are over, baby,
Night is drawing near,
Shadows of the evening crawl across the years.
You walk across the floor with your flower in your hand,
Trying to tell me no one understands,
Trading your hours for a handful of dimes,
Gonna make it, baby,
In our prime,
Get together one more time.

Get together one more time,
Get together one more time,
Get together one more time,
Get together one more time.

Well c'mon honey,
Get along home and wait for me.
Baby, I'll be home in just a little while.
Y'see, I gotta go out in this car
And...

Get together one more time,
Get together one more time,
Get together one more time,
Get together one more time.

Love you girl,
You're lookin' good.
Lookin' real good.
C'mon.

Yes The River Knows

The Doors

Please believe me,
The river told me,
Very softly
Want you to hold me.

Free fall flow river, flow,
On and on it goes,
Breathe under water till the end.

Free fall flow river, flow,
On and on it goes,
Breathe under water till the end.

Yes the river knows.

Please believe me,
If you don't need me
I'm going,
But I need a little time.

I promised I would drown myself
In mystic heated wine.

43

Please believe me,
The river told me
Very softly,
Want you to hold me.

I'm going but I need a little time,
I promised I would drown myself
In mystic heated wine.

Free fall flow river, flow,
On and on it goes,
Breathe under water till the end.

Free fall flow river, flow,
On and on it goes,
Breathe under water till the end.

The Unknown Soldier

The Doors

Wait until the war is over,
And we're both a little older.

The unknown soldier.

Practice where the news is read,
Television children dead,
Unborn, living,
Living, dead,
Bullet strikes the helmet's head.

And it's all over for the unknown soldier,
It's all over for the unknown soldier,
Uh uh.

"Company, halt!"

"Present Arms."

Make a grave for the unknown soldier,
Nestled in your hollow shoulder.

The unknown soldier.

Practice as the news is read,
Television children dead.

Bullet strikes the helmet's head.

It's all over,
The war is over.

Over.

Over.

My Wild Love

The Doors

My wild love went riding,
She rode all the day;
She rode to the devil,
And asked him to pay.

The devil was wiser.
It's time to repent;
He asked her to give back,
The money she spent.

My wild love went riding,
She rode to the sea;
She gathered together
Some shells for her hair.

She rode and she rode on
She rode for a while,
Then stopped for an evening
And laid her head down.

She rode on to Christmas,
She rode to the farm
She rode to Japan,
And re-entered a town.

By this time the weather
Had changed one degree,
She asked for the people
To let her go free.

My wild love went riding,
She rode for an hour;
She rode and she rested,
And then she rode on.

Easy Ride

Jim Morrison

And I know
It will be
An easy ride.
And I know
It will be
An easy ride.

The mask that you wore,
My fingers would explore
The costume of control
Excitement soon unfolds.

And I know
It will be
An easy ride
Joy fought vaguely
With your pride
With your pride

Like polished stone
Like polished stone
I see your eyes
Like burning glass
Like burning glass
I hear you smile
Smile babe

47

The mask that you wore
My fingers would explore
The costume of control
Excitement soon unfolds

And I know it will be
An easy ride

Coda queen – be my bride
Rage in darkness by my side
Seize the summer in your pride
Take the winter in your stride
Let's ride

Tell All The People

Robbie Krieger

Tell all the people that you see
Follow me,
Follow me down.

Tell all the people that you see
Set them free,
Follow me down.

You tell them they don't have to run,
We're gonna pick up everyone,
Come on, take me by the hand,
Gonna bury all our troubles in the sand.
Oh yeah!

Can't you see the wonder at your feet,
Your life's complete.
Follow me down
Can't you see me growing, get your guns,
The time has come,
To follow me down.

48

Follow me across the sea
Where milky babies seem to be molded flowing revelry
With the one that set them free.

Tell all the people that you see
It's just me,
Follow me down.

Tell all the people that you see,
Follow me,
Follow me down.

Tell all the people that you see,
We'll be free,
Follow me down.

Tell all the people that you see
It's just me,
Follow me down.

Tell all the people that you see,
Follow me,
Follow me down.

Follow me down,
You got to follow me down,
Follow me down.

Tell all the people that you see,
We'll be free,
Follow me down.

Touch Me

Robbie Krieger

C'mon, c'mon, c'mon, c'mon now,
Touch me, babe,
Can't you see that I am not afraid,
What was that promise that you made,
Why won't you tell me what she said,
What was that promise that she made.

Now I'm gonna love you till the heaven stops the rain,
I'm gonna love you till the stars fall from the sky,
For you and I.

C'mon, c'mon, c'mon, c'mon now,
Touch me, baby,
Can't you see that I am not afraid,
What was that promise that you made,
Why won't you tell me what she said,
What was that promise that she made.

I'm gonna love you till the heavens stop the rain,
I'm gonna love you till the stars fall from the sky,
For you and I.

49

I'm gonna love you till the heavens stop the rain,
I'm gonna love you till the stars fall from the sky,
For you and I.

Do It

Jim Morrison & Robbie Krieger

Yeah,
Please me,
Yeah,
Please, baby,
Please, please.

Please, please, listen to me children,
Please, please, listen to me children,
Please, please, listen to me children,
Please, please, listen to me children,
You are the ones who will rule the world.

Listen to me children,
Listen to me children,
Listen to me children,
Please, please, listen to me children,
You are the ones who will rule the world.

You gotta please me
All night.

50

Please, please, listen to me children,
Said please, please, listen to me children.
Please,
Yeah, please me.
I'm askin' you.

Please, please, listen to me children,
Please, please, listen to me children,
Please, please, listen to me children,
Please, my children,
Please, children.
Please,
Children.

Wild Child

The Doors

Wild child
Full of grace
Savior of the human race,
Your cool face.

Natural child,
Terrible child,
Not your mother's or your
Father's child.
You're our child,
Screamin' wild.

(An ancient lunatic reigns in the trees of the night.)

With hunger at her heels,
And freedom in her eyes,
She dances on her knees,
Pirate prince at her side.
Staring
Into
The hollow idol's eye.

51

Wild child,
Full of grace,
Savior of the human race,
Your cool face,
Your cool face,
Your cool face.

(You remember when we were in Africa?)

Shaman's Blues

Jim Morrison

There will never be another one
Like you.
There will never be another one who can
Do the things you do, Oh!
Will you give another chance?
Will you try a little try?
Please stop and you'll remember
We were together,
Anyway.

All right!

And, if you have a certain evening
You could lend to me,
I'll give it all right back to you.
Know how it has to be, with you.
I know you' moods,
And your mind,
And your mind,
And your mind,
And your mind,
And you're mine.

Will you stop and think and wonder
Just what you'll see,
Out on the train-yard
Nursing penitentiary.

It's gone,
I cry,
Out long.

Did you stop to consider
How it will feel,
Cold grinding' grizzly bear jaws
Hot on your heels.
Do you often stop and whisper
In Saturday's shore,
The whole world's a saviour,
And who could ever ever ever ever ever ever
Ask for more?

Do you remember?
Will you stop,
Will you stop, the pain?

There will never be another one
Like you.
There will never be another one who can
Do the things you do, Oh!
Will you give another chance?
Will you try a little try?
Please stop and you'll remember
We were together,
Anyway.

All right!

How you must think and wonder
How I must feel
Out on the meadows
While you're on the field.

I'm alone for you,
And I cry.

"He's sweatin', look at him... optical promise...
you'll be dead and in hell before I'm born...
sure thing... bridesmaid... the only solution...
isn't it amazing?"

Runnin' Blues

Robbie Krieger

Poor Otis dead and gone,
Left me here to sing his song,
Pretty little girl with the red dress on,
Poor Otis dead and gone.

Back down, turn around slowly,
Try it again,
Remembering when it was easy,
Try it again,
Much too easy – remembering when.

All right, look at my shoes,
Not quite the walkin' blues.
Don't fight, too much to lose,
Can't fight the runnin' blues.

Well, I've got the runnin' blues,
Runnin' away, back to L.A.
Got to find the dock on the bay,
Maybe find it in L.A.

Runnin' scared, runnin' blue,
Goin' so fast, what'll I do?

Well, I've got the runnin' blues,
Runnin' away, back to L.A.
Got to find the dock on the bay,
Maybe find it in L.A.

All right, look at my shoes,
Not quite the walkin' blues,
Don't fight, too much to lose,
Can't fight the runnin' blues.

Well, I've got the runnin' blues,
Runnin' away, back to L.A.
Got to find the dock on the bay,
Maybe find it in L.A.

Wishful Sinful

Robbie Krieger

Wishful sinful,
Water covers ev'rything in blue
Cooling water.

Wishful sinful, our love is beautiful to see,
I know where I would like to be:
Right back where I came.

Wishful sinful, wicked blue
Water covers you.
Can't escape the blue.

Magic rising,
Sun is shining deep beneath the sea.
But not enough for you and me and sunshine.

Love to hear the wind cry

Wishful sinful, our love is beautiful to see,
I know where I would like to be:
Right back where I came.

Wishful sinful, wicked blue
Water covers you.
Wishful sinful wicked blue
Can't escape the blue.

You and me and sunshine,
Love to hear the wind cry

Wishful sinful, our love is beautiful to see,
I know where I would like to be:
Right back where I came.

Wishful sinful, wicked blue,
Water covers you.
Can't escape the blue.

55

The Soft Parade

Jim Morrison

When I was back there in seminary school
There was a person there
Who put forth the proposition
That you can petition the Lord with prayer
Petition the Lord with prayer
Petition the Lord with prayer
You cannot petition the Lord with prayer!

Can you give me sanctuary
I must find a place to hide
A place for me to hide
Can you find me soft asylum
I can't make it any more
The man is at the door

Peppermint miniskirts, chocolate candy
Champion sax and a girl named Sandy

There's only four ways to get unraveled,
One is to sleep and the other is travel

One is a bandit up in the hills
One is to love your neighbor till
His wife gets home

Catacombs, nursery bones
Winter women growing stones
(Carrying babies to the river)

Streets and shoes, avenues
Leather riders selling news

(The monk bought lunch)

Successful hills are here to stay
Everything must be this way
Gentle street where people play
Welcome to the soft parade

All our lives we sweat and save
Building for a shallow grave
Must be something else we say
Somehow to defend this place
(Everything must be this way
Everything must be this way)

The soft parade has now begun
Listen to the engines hum
People out to have some fun
A cobra on my left
Leopard on my right

Deer woman in a silk dress
Girls with beads about their necks.
Kiss the hunter of the green vest
Who has wrestled before
With lions in the night

Out of sight!

The lights are getting brighter
The radio is moaning
Calling to the dogs
There are still a few animals
Left out in the yard
But it's getting harder
To describe
Sailors
To the underfed

Tropic corridor
Tropic treasure
What got us this far
To this mild Equator
We need something or something new
Something else to get us through.

Calling on the dogs
Calling on the dogs
Calling on the dogs
Calling in the dogs
Calling all the dogs
Calling on the dogs

Meet me at the crossroads
Meet me at the edge of town
Outskirts of the city
Just you and I
And the evening sky
You'd better come alone
You'd better bring your gun
We're gonna have some fun!

When all else fails,
We can whip the horses' eyes,
And make them sleep
And cry. . . . . .

MORRISON HOTEL /HARDROCK CAFÉ /1970

Roadhouse Blues

Jim Morrison

Keep your eyes on the road,
Keep your hands upon the wheel.
Keep your eyes on the road,
Your hands upon the wheel.
Yeah, we're goin' to the roadhouse,
Gonna have a real good time.

Yeah, in back of the roadhouse
They got some bungalows,
Yeah, in back of the roadhouse
They got some bungalows,
And that's for the people
Who like to go down slow.

Let it roll, baby, roll,
Let it roll, baby, roll,
Let it roll, baby, roll,
Let it roll,
All night long.

Ashen lady,
Ashen lady,
Give up your vows.
Give up your vows.

Save our city,
Save our city,
Right now!

When I woke up this mornin'
I got myself a beer,
When I woke up this mornin'
I got myself a beer.
The future's uncertain,
And the end is always near.

Let it roll, baby, roll,
Let it roll, baby, roll,
Let it roll, baby, roll,
Let it roll,
All night long.

You Make Me Real

Jim Morrison

I really want you,
Really do,
Really need you, baby,
God knows I do.
'Cause I'm not real enough without you;
Oh,
Oh, what can I do?

You make me real,
You make me feel
Like lovers feel.

I really want you,
Really do,
Really need you, baby,
Really do.
I'm not real enough without you;
Oh,
What can I do?

You make me real,
Only you, baby
Have that appeal.

So let me slide in your tender sunken sea,
Make me free, love,
Make me free.

Make me free,
You make me real.
You make me feel
Like lovers feel.

You make me throw away mistaken misery,
Make me free, love
Make me free.

Make me free
You make me free.

Blue Sunday

Jim Morrison

I found my own true love
Was on a blue Sunday.
She looked at me and told me
I was the only one in the world;
Now I have found my girl,
My girl awaits for me in tender time.
My girl is mine,
She is the world,
She is my girl.

My girl awaits for me in tender time,
My girl is mine,
She is the world,
She is my girl.

Land Ho!

Jim Morrison

Grand-Ma loved a sailor who sailed the frozen sea.
Grand-Pa was that whaler and he took me on his knee.
He said "Son, I'm goin' crazy from livin' on the land,
Got to find my shipmates and walk on foreign sands."

This old man was graceful, with silver in his smile.
He smoked a briar pipe and he walked our country miles.
Singing songs of shady sisters and old time liberty,
Songs of love and songs of death and songs to set me free.

I've got three ships and sixty men,
A course for ports unread.
I'll stand at mast, let north winds blow,
Till half of us are dead.

Land ho!

Well, if I get my hands on a dollar bill,
Gonna buy a bottle and drink my fill,
If I get my hands on a number five,
Gonna skin that little girl alive.

If I get my hands on a number two,
Come back home and marry you,
Marry you,
Marry you,
All right!

Land ho!
Land ho!
Land ho!
Land ho!
Land ho!
Land ho!
Land ho!

Waiting For The Sun

Jim Morrison

At first flash of Eden we raced down to the sea,
Standing there on freedom's shore.

Waiting for the sun,
Waiting for the sun,
Waiting for the sun.

Can't you feel it, now that spring has come,
That it's time to live in the scattered sun.

Waiting for the sun,
Waiting for the sun,
Waiting for the sun,
Waiting for the sun.

This is the strangest life I've ever known.

Can't you feel it, now that spring has come,
That it's time to live in the scattered sun.

Waiting for the sun,
Waiting for the sun,
Waiting for the sun.
Waiting for the sun.

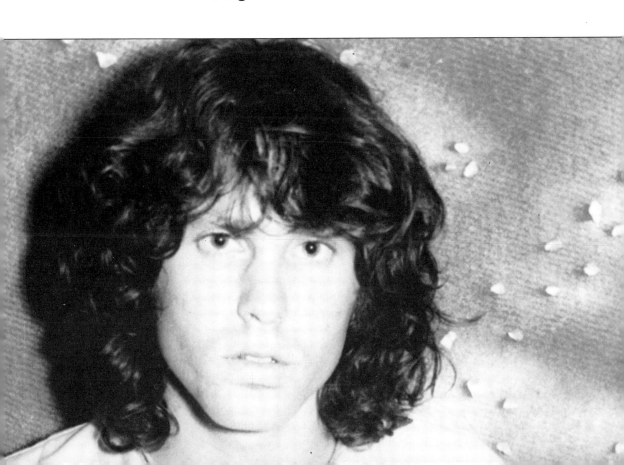

Ship of Fools

Jim Morrison

The human race was dying out,
No one left to scream and shout.
People walking on the moon,
Smog will get you pretty soon.

Ev'ryone was hangin' out,
Hangin' up and hangin' down,
Hangin' in and holdin' fast,
Hope our little world will last.

Along came Mister Goodtrips,
Looking for a new ship.
Come on, people, better climb on board,
Come on, baby, now we're going home.

Ship of fools,
Ship of fools.

The human race was dying out,
No one left to scream and shout.
People walking on the moon,
Smog gonna get you pretty soon.

Ship of fools,
Ship of fools,
Ship of fools.
Ship of fools
Ship of fools
Ship of fools
Ship of fools

Yeah, climb on board,
Ship's gonna leave y'all behind,
Climb on board.

Ship of fools,
Ship of fools.

Peace Frog

Jim Morrison

There's blood in the streets, it's up to my ankles,
Blood in the streets, it's up to my knee,
Blood in the streets of the town of Chicago,
Blood on the rise, it's following me.

Just about the break of day,
She came, then she drove away,
Sunlight in her hair.

Blood on the streets, runs a river of sadness,
Blood in the streets, it's up to my thigh.
The river runs down the legs of the city,
The women are crying red rivers of weeping.

She came in town and then she drove away,
Sunlight in her hair.

Indians scattered on dawn's highway bleeding,
Ghosts crowd the young child's fragile egg-shell mind.

Blood in the streets in the town of New Haven,
Blood stains the roofs and the palm trees of Venice,
Blood in my love in the terrible summer,
Bloody red sun of fantastic L.A.

Blood screams her brain as they chop off her fingers,
Blood will be born in the birth of a nation,
Blood is the rose of mysterious union.

There's blood in the streets it's up to my ankles,
Blood in the streets, it's up to my knee,
Blood in the streets of the town of Chicago,
Blood on the rise, it's following me.

Maggie M'Gill

Jim Morrison

Miss Maggie M'Gill she lived on a hill,
Her daddy got drunk and left her no will,
So she went down, down to "Tangie Town".
People down there really like to get it on.

Now, if you're sad and you're feelin' blue,
Go out and buy a brand new pair of shoes,
And you go down, down to "Tangle Town".
The people down there really like to get it on,
Get it on.

Illegitimate son of a rock and roll star
Illegitimate son of a rock and roll star
Mom met Dad in the back of a rock'n'roll car,
Yeah.

Well I'm an old blues man and I think that you understand,
I've been singing the blues ever since the world began.

66

Maggie,
Maggie,
Maggie M'Gill,
Roll on,
Roll on,
Maggie M'Gill.

Maggie,
Maggie,
Maggie M'Gill,
Roll on,
Roll on,
Maggie M'Gill.

Indian Summer

Jim Morrison & Robbie Krieger

I love you the best,
Better than all the rest,
I love you the best,
Better than all the rest,
That I meet in the summer,
Indian summer.
That I meet in the summer,
Indian summer.

I love you the best,
Better than all the rest.

Queen Of
The Highway

Jim Morrison & Robbie Krieger

She was a princess,
Queen of the highway.
Sign on the road said:
"Take us to Madre."
No one could save her,
Save the blind tiger.
He was a monster,
Black dressed in leather.

She was a princess,
Queen of the highway.

Now they are wedded,
She is a good girl,
Naked as children
Out in the meadow.
Naked as children,
Wild as can be,
Soon to have offspring,
Start it all over,
Start it all over.

American boy,
American girl,
Most beautiful people in the world!
Son of a frontier Indian Swirl,
Dancing thru the midnight whirl-pool,
Formless
Hope it can continue a little while longer.

The Spy

Jim Morrison

I'm a spy in the house of love,
I know the dream that you're dreamin' of,
I know the word that you long to hear,
I know your deepest secret fear.

I'm a spy in the house of love,
I know the dream that you're dreamin' of,
I know the word that you long to hear,
I know your deepest secret fear.

I know ev'rything,
Ev'rything you do,
Ev'rywhere you go,
Ev'ryone you know.

I'm a spy in the house of love,
I know the dream that you're dreamin' of.
I know the word that you long to hear,
I know your deepest secret fear.

I know your deepest secret fear,
I know your deepest secret fear.
I'm a spy,
I can see you
What you do;
And I know.

69

Changeling

Jim Morrison, The Doors

I live up town,
I live down-town,
I live all around.

I had money,
I had none,
I had money,
I had none;
But I never been so broke that I couldn't leave town.

I'm a changeling,
See me change.
I'm a changeling,
See me change.

I'm the air you breathe,
Food you eat,
Friends you greet
In the swarming street.

See me change,
See me change.

I live up town,
I live down-town,
I live all around.

I had money, yeah,
I had none,
I had money, yeah,
I had none;
But I never been so broke that I couldn't leave town.

I'm the air you breathe,
Food you eat,
Friends you greet
In the swarming street.

See me change,
See me change.

I'm leaving town,
On the midnight train,
Gonna see me change, change, change.

Change, change, change.
Change, change, change.

Love Her Madly

Robbie Krieger

Don't you love her madly?
Don't you need her badly?
Don't you love her ways?
Tell me what you say?
Don't you love her madly?
Want to be her daddy?
Don't you love her face?
Don't you love her as she's walking out the door?
Like she did one thousand times before.
Don't you love her ways?
Tell me what you say,
Don't you love her as she's walking out the door?

All your love, all your love,
All your love, all your love,
All your love is gone,
So sing a lonely song
Of a deep blue dream,
Seven horses seem
To be on the mark.

Yeah, don't you love her?
Don't you love her as she's walking out the door?

All your love, all your love,
All your love, all your love,
All your love is gone,
So sing a lonely song
Of a deep blue dream,
Seven horses seem
To be on the mark.

Don't you love her madly?
Don't you love her madly?
Don't you love her madly?

Been Down
So Long

Jim Morrison

Well, I been down so God-damn long,
That it looks like up to me.
Well, I been down so very damn long,
That it looks like up to me.
Now, why don't one of you people
C'mon and set me free?

I said warden, warden, warden,
Won't you break your lock and key,
I said warden, warden, warden,
Won't you break your lock and key.
Hey, come along here, mister,
C'mon and let the poor boy be.

Baby, baby, baby,
Won't you get down on your knees
Baby, baby, baby,
Won't you get down on your knees
C'mon little darlin',
C'mon and give your love to me.
Oh, yeah.

Well, I been down so God-damn long,
That it looks like up to me.
Well, I been down so very damn long,
That it looks like up to me.
Now why don't one of you people
C'mon, c'mon, c'mon
And set me free!

L.A. Woman

Jim Morrison

Well, I just got into town about an hour ago,
Took a look around, see which way the wind blow,
Where the little girls in their Hollywood bungalows,
Are you a lucky little lady in the city of light?
Or just another lost angel.

City of night,
City of night,
City of night,
City of night.

L.A. woman, L.A. woman,
L.A. woman, Sunday afternoon,
L.A. woman, Sunday afternoon.

L.A. woman, Sunday afternoon,
Drive thru your suburbs,
Into your blues,
Into your blues,
Into your blue, blue, blues,
Into your blues.

I see your hair is burning,
Hills are filled with fire;
If they say I never loved you,
You know they are a liar.

Drivin' down the freeway,
Midnight alleys roam,
Cops in cars, the topless bars,
Never saw a woman so alone,
So alone, so alone, so alone.

Motel money,
Murder madness,
Let's change the mood
From glad to sadness.

Mister Mojo risin'
Mister Mojo risin'
Mister Mojo risin'
Mister Mojo risin'
Got to keep on risin'
Mister Mojo risin'
Mister Mojo risin'
Mojo risin'
Got the Mojo risin'
Mister Mojo risin'
Got to keep on risin'

Risin', risin',
Risin', risin',
Risin', risin',
Risin', risin',
Risin', risin',

Well, I just got into town about an hour ago,
Took a look around, see which way the wind blow,
Where the little girls in their Hollywood bungalows,
Are you a lucky little lady in the city of light?
Or just another lost angel.

City of night,
City of night,
City of night,
City of night.

L.A. woman, L.A. woman,
L.A. woman,
You're my woman.

L.A. woman, L.A. woman,
She's my woman,
L.A. woman.

L'America

Jim Morrison

I took a trip down to L'America
To trade some beads for a pint of gold.
I took a trip down to L'America
To trade some beads for a pint of gold.

L'America, L'America,
L'America, L'America,
L'America, L'America.

C'mon people, don't you look so down;
You know the rainman's comin' to town.
He'll change your weather,
He'll change your luck,
Then he'll teach you how to find yourself,
L'America.

Friendly strangers came to town,
All the people put them down,
But the women loved their ways,
Come again some other day.
Like the gentle rain,
Like the gentle rain that falls.

I took a trip down to L'America,
To trade some beads for a pint of gold.
I took a trip down to L'America,
To trade some beads for pint of gold.

L'America, L'America,
L'America, L'America,
L'America, L'America,
L'America.

Cars Hiss By
My Window

Jim Morrison

The cars hiss by my window,
Like the waves down on the beach.
The cars hiss by my window,
Like the waves down on the beach.
I got this girl beside me,
But she's out of reach.

Headlights thru my window,
Shining on the wall.
Headlights thru my window,
Shining on the wall.
Can't hear my baby,
Tho' I call and call.

Window started tremblin',
With those sonic boom.
Window started to tremble,
With those sonic boom, boom.
A cold girl'll kill you
In a darkened room.

The Wasp

Jim Morrison

I want to tell you about Texas Radio and the big beat.
It comes out of the Virginia swamps,
Cool and slow, with precision, with a back beat,
Narrow and hard to master.
Some call it heavenly in its brilliance,
Others, mean and rueful of the Western dream,
I love the friends I have gathered together on this thin raft,
We have constructed pyramids in honor of our escaping.
This is the land where the Pharaoh died.

The Negroes in the forest, brightly feathered,
And they are saying:
"Forget the night! Live with us in forests of azure,
Out here on the perimeter, there are no stars:
Out here we is stoned – immaculate."

Listen to this I'll tell you about the heartaches,
I'll tell you about the heartaches and the loss of God.
I'll tell you about the hopeless night,
The meager food the souls forgot,
Tell you about the maiden with wrought iron soul.

I'll tell you this
No eternal reward can forgive us now,
For wasting the dawn.

I'll tell you about Texas Radio and the big beat,
Soft-driven, slow and mad like some new language.

Now listen to this I'll tell you about Texas,
I'll tell you about Texas Radio,
I'll tell you about the hopeless night,
The wanderin' the Western dream,
Tell you about the maiden with wrought iron soul.

Hyacinth House

Jim Morrison

What are they doing in the Hyacinth house,
What are they doing in the Hyacinth house
To please the lions this day?

I need a brand new friend who doesn't bother me,
I need a brand new friend who doesn't trouble me.
I need someone
Who doesn't need me.

I see the bathroom is clear,
I think that somebody's near,
I'm sure that someone is following me.
Oh, yeah.

Why did you throw the Jack-of-Hearts away?
Why did you throw the Jack-of-Hearts away?
It was the only card in the deck that I had left to play.

And I'll say it again,
I need a brand new friend,
And I'll say it again,
I need a brand new friend,
And I'll say it again,
I need a brand new friend,
The end.

Riders On
The Storm

Jim Morrison

Riders on the storm,
Riders on the storm,
Into this house we're born,
Into this world we're thrown,
Like a dog without a bone,
An actor out on loan,
Riders on the storm.

There's a killer on the road,
His brain is squirming like a toad.
Take a long holiday
Let your children play.
If you give this man a ride,
Sweet family will die.
Killer on the road.

Girl you gotta love your man,
Girl you gotta love your man.
Take him by the hand,
Make him understand,
The world on you depends,
Our life will never end,
You gotta love your man.

Riders on the storm,
Riders on the storm,
Into this house we're born,
Into this house we're thrown,
Like a dog without a bone,
An actor out on loan,
Riders on the storm.

Riders on the storm,
Riders on the storm,
Riders on the storm,
Riders on the storm.

2/93 (17176)